There's really nothing special or noteworthy about Michael Holmes, just a simple man. But this book might say a lot about the author. Actually, the stars of the book are the wildlife, who brought great enjoyment to him. He also thinks it is nice to see others, young and old alike, find the same enjoyment.

Michael Holmes remembers when he and his mother were taking photographs of a black bear that had a blonde coloring. They ended up watching the bear for about an hour and it was amazing how many people stopped to take photos. Since there was no place to park along the highway, some drove slow while trying to capture some photos. The experience was unforgettable.

The AMAZING ZOO
IN MY BACKYARD

MICHAEL HOLMES

AUSTIN MACAULEY PUBLISHERS™
LONDON • CAMBRIDGE • NEW YORK • SHARJAH

Ordering Information
Quantity sales: Special discounts are available on quantity purchases by corporations, associations, and others. For details, contact the publisher at the address below.

Publisher's Cataloging-in-Publication data
Holmes, Michael
The Amazing Zoo in My Backyard

ISBN 9781645754350 (Paperback)
ISBN 9781645754343 (Hardback)
ISBN 9781645754367 (ePub e-book)

Library of Congress Control Number: 2021923478

www.austinmacauley.com/us

First Published 2024
Austin Macauley Publishers LLC
40 Wall Street, 33rd Floor, Suite 3302
New York, NY 10005
USA

mail-usa@austinmacauley.com
+1 (646) 5125767

To my mother, Judy.
After all it is her backyard, which thrills her that so many wildlife have become visitors to the amazing zoo year after year. It was also my mother who penned the name "Backyard Zoo" giving me the idea to write the book, which has brought me so much enjoyment. It is also my mother's favorite book.
For this, I am very appreciative and grateful. Many thanks and all my love to my parents.

To everyone who has given me so many wonderful compliments for the photographs that I have shown them and for the first book that was published. The words are so encouraging and appreciated. I would love to name everyone but the list would be too long but I will not forget and it is my desire that everyone will find as much enjoyment in this book, as I did in photographing and watching the amazing wildlife in the backyard.

Table of Contents

Birds

When I hear the word zoo, my imagination immediately goes to a variety of amazing wildlife that are either penned up in cages or are fenced in, so that we can enjoy these amazing animals and birds that we do not have the opportunity or the circumstances to enjoy or even see.

How about this amazing grizzly bear that was rescued and because it was, we can watch and photograph it.

It is certainly worth the time to visit these amazing places. I was certainly glad that I took the time to visit these amazing places, but as always, I sure wished that I had taken more time to enjoy these amazing wildlife that can be found.

I was delighted to see such amazing animals as a hippopotamus or a giraffe. Even to be able to see a red panda makes me want to go back to a zoo again and again, but this time I will definitely take a lot more time so that I can fully enjoy the beauty of all the wildlife that is found in a zoo.

But it is of interest to know that one can also have and enjoy a zoo in one's own backyard. At least, this is what my mother now calls her backyard because of the wide variety of birds and other animals that we have been able to enjoy and photograph.

All that it takes is to put up a few bird feeders and to spent roughly, but conservatively, around 700 dollars a years on bird feed. From the bags of sunflower seeds to the bells made of sunflower seeds. Of course, I can't forget the peanuts which is the favorite food for these very special birds and animals.

Naturally, I don't mind it one bit to spend this much because it gives me much enjoyment and pleasure as I take so many amazing photographs of the amazing wildlife that can be found in a backyard.

You may not see a Canada lynx like this one in your backyard, but it has been amazing to see well over sixty different variety of birds and even wildlife that you may not even expect to see, but are still a pleasure to see and take so many amazing photographs of.

It is also certainly a joy to be able to go out into the backyard and see as many as fifty to possibly as many as a hundred and fifty birds at one time. I have even seen as many as seven or eight different birds on any particular day. Wow!

It even makes my day when I see a particular bird, such as a red crossbill show up. But, not just a few of them, I am able to see as many as thirty or possibly even more than this. Yes, some birds seem to come in by the flock.

What a thrill!

But let me get back to the beginning and why I started to feed and enjoy the amazing birds that can be seen and enjoyed even in a backyard.

It all started one fall day when I noticed a blue jay in the backyard that was next to my parents. You see there is an oak tree in their backyard and I just happened to see it eating the acorns that had fallen to the ground.

It was probably a blue jay like this one.

It was truly incredible to watch this beautiful bird as it hopped from one acorn to the next one. I was hooked!

So I thought it would be a good idea to start feeding the birds to see how many I would be able to attract into my parent's backyard so that I would be able to get some amazing photographs.

It worked! It wasn't very long before a blue jay had noticed the feeder and started to eat the seeds each day after that. Yes, with this small beginning, I was certainly happy to end up with what my mother ends up calling, her amazing backyard zoo.

What also makes this backyard zoo such an amazing one is that I am able to enjoy many other animals besides the incredible birds.

From rabbits to even a red fox that went walking past. From white-tailed deer to the many other animals that are enjoyable to watch. But, at times though, we see the unwanted birds and animals as well, such as a coyote and even a merlin and a sharp-shinned hawk which chases the other birds away from time to time.

Even though these ones disrupt the backyard zoo from time to time, there is nothing that I can do, but to take the time to photograph these as well.

So I hope that you will enjoy the amazing wildlife as I give you a personal tour of our backyard zoo, even this one that is found in a city, like my mother's.

Blue Jay

Let's start the tour with what is my favorite bird in the backyard zoo and it is by far the bird that I have photographed the most. Why not?

I would have to say that it is the most colorful of all the birds that have shown up in our zoo. It is probably because of the vivid colors. It also doesn't hurt that blue is my favorite color, but it is more than that. Just the sheer variety of color that makes the blue jay such a beautiful bird. From the different shades of blue and then, you add the colors of black and white and the color gray, it makes the blue jay the most beautiful of all birds. That is my opinion, of course.

I can sit for hours just watching this amazing bird as it scoops up peanuts and sunflower seeds by the beak full. I actually have a photograph of a blue jay with four peanuts that can be clearly seen in its beak.

Peanuts are by far the blue jay's favorite food, if it is given a choice. But, left with just sunflower seeds, it is certainly an enjoyable experience to be able to watch a blue jay pick up a few seeds and then, to have it fly into a tree and crack the seeds. What a treat! Simply amazing.

One day it was nice to see a family of three blue jays stop by and visit the backyard and with each passing year, the blue jay is a regular visitor to the backyard zoo during all seasons.

But even though the blue jay is a beautiful bird it makes a horrible noise, a loud shriek. A not so friendly sound to our ears, but I don't pay all that much attention to its sound as I am in awe because of its sheer beauty!

Red-Breasted Nuthatch

Another interesting bird that I have enjoyed watching and taking so many amazing photographs of is a red-breasted nuthatch.

It's amazing to see them fly onto the feeder and take a peanut or a sunflower seed, but not just any peanut will do. They will pick one and if it is not satisfactory, they will drop it and go on to the next one. They will keep looking until they find one that is and then, they will fly away into a tree to eat their food.

It is very noticeable how careful they are when they come for a peanut, especially if the feeder is full of birds. They will wait for a convenient opportunity to get their meal and when there is an opening, they will swoop in.

Occasionally though, they don't get a peanut when they fly in because before they can get a peanut, another bird flies in and chases the red-breasted nuthatch away. But it waits until it is finally successful.

To my amazement, it isn't long before it is back for seconds and thirds.

Spending the whole day as they take more and more peanuts. It actually makes me wonder if they are storing them for a rainy day or to get as many peanuts and seeds before they think that all the peanuts or seeds are gone.

Foolish bird! They should know by now that there is an inexhaustible supply of bird seed.

At one very special time when I was placing a handful of peanuts on the platform that I use as a bird feeder, a red-breasted nuthatch was in no hurry to fly away. It just sat there on an oak tree branch.

Could this prove to be a very special opportunity and what could have been a very thrilling experience?

I was not going to let this opportunity slip away. Being brave, I decided to see if the red-breasted nuthatch would take a peanut out of my hand.

To my amazement, the red-breasted nuthatch flew right up to my hand and just hovered there for a moment. It certainly came close, certainly tempted. But, sadly I must have flinched just a little because the bird quickly flew back into the oak tree.

Even though I was utterly unsuccessful, I was still going to keep trying. You never know what can happen, the amazing possibilities are endless! Sure enough, I had an amazing experience with a red-breasted nuthatch. To my utter surprise, it happened on a very special day. When I take photograph of the birds as they come to feed on the feeders, I place my chair only about six to ten feet away. This is so that I can get the most amazing photographs that are possible.

Well, as I was waiting to take photographs of the blue jays that were coming to get the peanuts on the feeder, I had a red-breasted nuthatch land on my knee. What a thrill!

Sadly, though there were two red-breasted nuthatches in the backyard because another one chased him off my knee. Who knows just how long that red-breasted nuthatch might have stayed on my knee.

What an amazing and incredible photograph that would have made! Thankfully, I have the memory of this very special moment. That is what happens when you are not prepared for the unexpected. You miss out on some incredible opportunities to get some amazing photographs.

Another thing that makes watching the red-breasted nuthatch so enjoyable is when there is two or more of them in the backyard zoo. That is because no matter how much of an abundance of seeds and peanuts there is, there is always one joker that has to hoard all the food by chasing the other red-breasted nuthatch away.

But, for all the good that does because after the red-breasted nuthatch thinks that the rest of them have been chased away, it gets its peanut and flies away.

In the meantime, as this red-breasted nuthatch is away, the others come back and get their peanuts. Ha! Ha! Ha! The joke was on him.

Blue-Headed Vireo

One thing about a flycatcher like a blue-headed vireo is that they are awfully hard to get a photograph of.

That is why I was totally thrilled when I was able to get an amazing photograph of this colorful blue-headed vireo.

One thing that makes this backyard zoo such an amazing zoo is that it is about a half-an-acre and there is a lot of trees in the yard.

Well, one beautiful evening as I was strolling around the backyard, I came across this amazing bird and even though, this blue-headed vireo was on a tree that was on the boundary of the backyard zoo, it was no problem.

There was no fence so I just walked around the tree and making sure that the sun was in the best position as was possible, I was able to get an amazing photograph of this incredible bird, a blue-headed vireo.

I was certainly happy that this amazing bird was able to poise for me just long enough so that I could get the photograph. Thanks a bunch!

Ruby-Throated Hummingbird

It is truly a remarkable thing to be able to spend time watching and enjoying this tiny, but amazing bird. I certainly appreciate the time, sometimes it maybe for only a brief moment, but I am certainly in awe of this incredible ruby-throated hummingbird.

I first noticed the ruby-throated hummingbird by accident. All I saw was something flash by in the distance and upon a closer inspection, I soon realized what it was. A ruby-throated hummingbird.

On one very beautiful evening I was able to watch this very small, but really fast bird as it flew from one flower to the next flower. Aha! Now that I had seen one, I was going to get a photograph of them as I ended up seeing a couple of ruby-throated hummingbirds.

The next evening, I was able to get a few photographs. I probably stood and watched them for around two and a half hours to maybe three hours.

As you can see from the photograph it looks like the ruby-throated hummingbird has three wings. It just shows just fast that a ruby-throated hummingbird flaps its wings.

At about the rate of up to eighty times per second, it is easy to see why there are three wings in the photograph. Now that is fast and just proves what an incredible bird that the ruby-throated hummingbird is.

It is simply amazing to see the ruby-throated hummingbird just hoover in empty space. Such grace and beauty can only make one just stand there in awe. When a ruby-throated hummingbird decides to leave to find other flowers in which to drink their nectar, there gone. In the blink of an eye, a ruby-throated hummingbird can fly across this backyard zoo. It is amazing just how fast that they can fly away, so fast that it seems that they can do it in the blink of an eye.

It is too bad that I am not able to show you a male ruby-throated hummingbird so that you can see how this amazing bird got its name. But I am hoping that eventually I will be able to get an amazing photograph of a male ruby-throated hummingbird so that you can see his amazing red throat.

I will have to start looking for a ruby-throated hummingbird early in the year as this is probably the best time to find a male one.

American Sparrows

Another variety of birds that are seen quite often in the backyard are American sparrows.

Most days you can see white-crowned sparrows and house sparrows and white-throated sparrows, chipping sparrows, Harris's sparrows and I was even able to see a fox sparrow.

American sparrows are another bird that when they move in, they move in by the flock. I have seen as many as thirty or more sparrows at one time and with each passing year I am able to see more and more of them. To the point that there seems to be over a hundred of them.

Yes, there are so numerous that when I am walking home, I can hear them chirping even though I am still about a block away. It also doesn't take long for them to go through a gallon of seeds. Of course, it doesn't take them long to empty the lighthouse bird feeder as they shovel most of the seeds on the ground which gives even more sparrows an opportunity to feed from the bird seed.

I don't mind this one bit because for the tens of tens of bags of seeds that I put out, not much is wasted. The pile on the ground doesn't get very high.

White-Throated Sparrow

Chipping Sparrow

Even though some may view American sparrows as plain looking because their color is just brown. A color that doesn't make a bird stand out by any stretch of the imagination. When you consider that they are at the bottom of the food chain, they need all the help that they can get.

But, a closer inspection of the many American sparrows that visit my backyard zoo, they do have a variety of color that also makes them a beautiful bird. They have such colors as white and black and even differing shades of brown. I guess that I shouldn't forget the color yellow.

The things that makes me watch these American sparrows is how they look after their young ones like this chipping sparrow.

It doesn't matter where the parent may fly to their offspring is hot on their heels. When they catch up to the parent you can see the offspring with their mouth wide open and if that is not enough to catch their attention, the offspring begins to start shaking and shaking.

It is really cute looking when you see so many of them following the parents from tree to tree trying their best to get the attention of their parents.

White-Crowned Sparrow

Harris's Sparrow

Fox Sparrow

House Sparrow

American Redstart

This was the hardest bird in which to photograph. But, as with everything it just takes a little patience and you will eventually get an amazing photograph.

As I was sitting outside one day, trying to get a photograph of any beautiful bird that might show up, two female American redstarts flew into the backyard zoo.

I was really disappointed that I was unable to get an amazing photograph of them. It was because they were jumping from branch to branch so quickly that they never gave me enough time so that I could take a photograph.

But I was very happy that I was finally able to get this amazing photograph of an American redstart. But it was quite a chore just to get this one.

instead of the yellow color of a female. Even being able to get a photograph of an American redstart with its tail feathers fanned out as it hops around a tree trying to get some insects to eat. Just beautiful!

Downy Woodpecker

It is interesting how a bird will react when they are in danger.

It happened on a particular day when I looked out the window to see what birds just happened to be in my backyard zoo. The only bird I saw in the backyard was a downy woodpecker. That fact alone should have been a clue that something was up. But, I didn't get it. Wow!

But the way that the downy woodpecker was acting caught my curiosity. You see, the downy woodpecker was hugging the trunk of the oak tree and was also looking up into a maple tree.

I thought that this would make for an incredible opportunity to take a photograph. So I went and got my camera and headed outside.
Well, needless to say, I quickly noticed why the downy woodpecker was so motionless.

Yes, it didn't take me long, only a few seconds when I noticed a sharp shinned hawk sitting in the maple tree.

Obviously, sometimes you can get a guest in one's backyard that is ,unwelcomed, but more about this subject later. It is also amazing how instinctively wise a bird is when it comes to their survival.

Needless to say, I chased the sharp-shinned hawk away so that the downy woodpecker could fly away safely.

One thing that any woodpecker enjoys to eat is a bell made out of sunflower seeds. They just sit on the bell and pounds away with his beak to get to the seeds. It is amazing to watch a downy woodpecker do this for hours.

When it comes to their ,food, some birds get very protective. Even though, there is plenty of seeds, enough for everyone. But, for some reason certain birds do not want to share.

As I was watching a downy woodpecker one day, this is exactly what happened. A downy woodpecker was on the bell and pecking away when all of a sudden, he was interrupted. Well, of all the nerve!

A pine siskin had landed on the bell as well, obviously to eat. This did not make the downy woodpecker happy.

First, he tried to stare him down or should I say off the bell. That wasn't going to work. So after a minute or so passed, the downy woodpecker got mean. He tried to peck him off. It worked!

Once was enough, the pine siskin got the hint and soon realized that the downy woodpecker was in no mood to share and flew away.

Happy now, the downy woodpecker went back to getting at his food.

I just wished that I could have taken the photograph of the two birds on the bell as the downy woodpecker was staring down the pine siskin.

Hairy Woodpecker

When you see a hairy woodpecker, you quickly notice that they are not much different than a downy woodpecker. Actually, the only thing that makes the two stand out as different is the size of their beaks. The hairy woodpecker has a much larger beak.

But, just like the downy woodpecker, they also like to eat the sunflower seeds that make up a bell. With that huge beak they can sure whittle down that bell. Yes, before you know it that bell is gone. Wow, now that is amazing.

One time that I remember fondly is when the bell eventually fell down and was laying on the ground. Needless to say, this did not make any difference to the hairy woodpecker. It just ate from the bell as it was laying on the ground.

What was interesting enough is that the bell landed next to the platform bird feeder. As the hairy woodpecker was on the bell a house sparrow landed on the platform to have some of the seeds that were on it.

This did not go over very well for the hairy woodpecker and he just sat there and stared at the house sparrow. It certainly made for an interesting and amazing photograph.

I also find it very interesting how the hairy woodpecker uses its tail as a way to balance himself as it pecks and eats the sunflower seeds on the bell.

Simply amazing!

Brown-Headed Cowbird

This is an interesting bird with a very unusual name, but it was a pleasant surprise to come across this amazing bird.

I was quite surprised just how close I was able to get to this bird. Even though, it was not eating it just sat on a branch and poised for me. I am very appreciative for the help that I was able to receive in taking an amazing photograph of a brown-headed cowbird.

Happily, I have seen this amazing bird many times. Yes, a brown-headed cowbird is a frequent visitor to the lighthouse bird feeder.

It gave me many opportunities to try to get an amazing photograph of this bird. Of course, the best opportunity came when a merlin suddenly appeared in the backyard zoo.

The only place that is a safe place for the birds are the trees. When danger comes, they immediately fly up into the tree and they stay perched on a branch until the danger has passed and the merlin has flown away.

When I saw the brown-headed cowbird flew into the pine tree in the yard because of the merlin, I went to see if this is exactly what happened. It was.

Yes, the brown-headed cowbird was not going to go anywhere, no matter how close I walked up to where he was sitting. This gave me many amazing photographs and when I had taken a few photograph I left.

Brown Creeper

This is a bird that I have never seen before and the only reason that I even was able to see this bird was because it moved.

These amazing photographs of this brown creeper show why it is so very hard to see them. They blend in very good with the bark of a tree. Yes, if a brown creeper did not move you probably would not even see them. Almost to the point that they are almost invisible.

Wow, what an amazing, natural and very good defense against anything that might bring them harm that they have.

When I saw a brown creeper for the first time, I just happened to be walking past a tree when it flew from one tree to the other one. This immediately caught my attention.

I proceeded to follow it from tree to tree, all the while taking some amazing photographs in the process.

Yes, what a unique and amazing bird!

Hermit Thrush

One of the things that I enjoy doing is to sit outside on a sunny day and see if I can get any amazing photographs of the birds that happen to fly into my backyard zoo. I may have to sit outside for many hours, but usually my patience is rewarded.

This happened one day while I was sitting and taking photographs of some of the birds that came to feed on the sunflower seeds that I give to the birds to eat.

To my sure delight and pleasure, a hermit thrush just happened to fly into the oak tree. This opportunity gave me an amazing photograph of the hermit thrush as he was deciding if he should fly down to the sunflower seeds that were on the platform that was just below the oak tree.

The hermit thrush finally decided not to have any sunflower seeds, but I was delighted that the hermit thrush did not fly away. He just flew into a flower patch that was beside the house and I was able to get an even more amazing photograph.

Yellow-Bellied Sapsucker

Something that really helps when it comes to taking a photograph of the amazing birds that show up in a backyard zoo is trying to keep out of sight. Even if it means that one has to hide behind a tree or even in the bushes.

I noticed one day while I was out in the backyard a yellow-bellied sapsucker landed on a maple tree. The maple tree just happened to be near a nice lilac hedge. I took advantage of this amazing opportunity.

The first thing that I tried to do was to try to take a photograph from behind the lilac hedge. I was able to accomplish my goal and was successful.

As always, I try to get even closer and therefore, get even more incredible photographs. Since the yellow-bellied sapsucker didn't seem to be too concerned with what I was doing, I decided to walk around the lilac hedge and see if I could get closer.

I was able to get very close and get an amazing photograph of the yellowbellied sapsucker as he was way too busy in getting at the sap from the maple tree.

After I took my photographs of this incredible bird, I ended up just sitting there and watching this yellow-bellied sapsucker hop around the maple tree as it was looking for the sap coming out of the hole that it had made in the truck. The sure colorful beauty of the yellow-bellied sapsucker had me in awe.

Northern Flicker

When you see a northern flicker, a yellow shafted form, you notice that they are not the most beautiful bird, but they are still very enjoyable to watch. Especially when they are digging into the ground for their food because it looks like their whole head is in the ground.

One day, as I was walking in the meadow that is beside the backyard, I came across a couple of northern flickers. Since this was early in the year, the two northern flickers were obviously young and carefree.

The reason that they were so carefree was because they were so busy looking for their food that they paid no attention to what I was doing. Sneaking up on them so that I could get an amazing photograph was not going to be a problem at all.

Needless to say, the mother certainly did notice what I was doing. The closer that I got to the young ones on the ground, I heard the mother up in a tree nearby giving out a loud warning call.

As I got closer and closer, the louder and more frequent the warning calls came, but it didn't matter.

It was certainly a good thing that I wasn't a hawk for the sake of these innocent and foolish birds.

The best photographs that I was able to get of a northern flicker is when the northern flicker is so busy that you can sneak up on them quite easily.

One day, when there was still snow on the ground except for the small patches of grass showing, I noticed one in the front yard. I immediately got my camera and headed outside before it flew away.

Well, I certainly didn't need to worry about sneaking up on the northern flicker because it was so busy trying to get to the worm that it was not going to fly away. I was totally ignored, but that was okay as I got my amazing photo.

I was very fortunate to be able to get an amazing photograph of a northern flicker this year and it was all because I hid behind an elm tree.
I was thrilled when I saw a couple of northern flicker, but I wondered how was I going to get a photograph of them. Well, before they noticed me, I was able to sneak behind the tree.

Now here is where patience came into play. I just stood behind the tree for what seemed to be quite a while and hoping that I would be able to get an amazing photograph.

They were too busy hopping all around the yard trying to get their food. They just kept getting closer and closer until finally they got so close that I was able to get the best photograph that I was ever able to get of a northern flicker.

Red Crossbill

What a surprise and a joy it was when the red crossbills showed up in the backyard zoo. It was certainly an unexpected surprise since I had never seen any red crossbills before.

It was also amazing just how many of them flew into the backyard. I stopped counting at thirty-nine on and around the platform feeder and that is not even counting the many more red crossbills sitting in the oak tree and on the pine trees that are just behind the oak tree. It is easy to say that there was probably fifty or even more than that.

Boy, could they eat.

That bell made of sunflower seeds that they are sitting on. In just a few days it was gone. Not to mention the half a gallon or so of sunflower seeds that I put out on a platform feeder. By late afternoon it was gone too.

Once in a while I was putting out two feedings of sunflower seeds a day because they were going through the seeds so fast. Now, that is a lot of sunflower seeds to feed this flock of red crossbills.

What a privilege it was to see these amazing birds every day!

But it seems that as good as things get, all good things come to an end eventually. Yes, as quickly as they flew in, they left just as quickly.

Although, I will have to admit, they did not leave on their own.

As I was sitting outside and enjoying them eat at the feeders, when all of a sudden that feeling of joy was abruptly turned into shock when a sharpshinned hawk came flying in out from nowhere and caught one of the red crossbills.

Yes, sadly after this event, all the red crossbills flew away and never returned to the backyard zoo again.

Disappointed?

Without a doubt. I really found a lot of pleasure in watching and taking so many amazing photographs of these incredible birds, the red crossbills.

I am going to be very hopeful that I will be seeing these incredible red crossbills again, but only time will tell.

It will certainly be a delight if I am able to see them this fall or the early part of winter.

You see I can never have enough amazing photographs of the incredible visitors to the backyard zoo. This would include the amazing red crossbills.

Black-Capped Chickadee

When I first took a photograph of a black-capped chickadee, I was amazed that it was on the rough side and so scrawny looking. But, as you can see from these amazing photographs, these black-capped chickadees do not have that problem. They are beautiful looking in appearance because they are very well fed. I am certainly glad that I can help these amazing birds out.

These black-capped chickadees love to get a peanut from the platform feeder and then, just sit on a branch to eat its peanut.

I was even privileged to have a black-capped chickadee land on my hand when I held it out with peanuts in it. But, the black-capped chickadee took off too quickly and didn't take a peanut.

I will just have to keep trying until the black-capped chickadee gets comfortable enough with me, so that they will take a peanut from my hand. There is certainly enough of them. Surely I can get at least one of them to give me the incredible thrill of being able to feed them from my hand. Just have to be patient, but I know that day will arrive.

Now, that would be an amazing experience!

Pine Siskin

Cedar Waxwing

Bohemian Waxwing

It is amazing just how close a cedar waxwing and a bohemian waxwing look alike. That is probably why they have the same last name, since they are so similar. The only difference between the two birds is the yellow belly of the cedar waxwing and the gray belly of the bohemian waxwing.

The other difference is the bohemian waxwing is around for the winter and the cedar waxwing is smarter and heads south for the winter. Smart bird!

You can certainly tell when bohemian waxwings are around. Just take a look at the trees that have berries on them, like a mountain ash as an example. It doesn't take them long to clean a tree of its berries, but what do you expect when they come in by a flock.

I can remember one time, when I saw a flock of bohemian waxwing as they took turns eating berries on a mountain ash. When they were done, they flew back into another tree. Then, it was someone else's turn and then, they flew into the mountain ash for their food. This went on for quite some time.

I patiently watched them for a while and after, I had taken my amazing photographs, I left.

It was amazing to me that when I walked past that mountain ash the following day or it could have been a day later, the berries on the mountain ash were gone. It was picked clean, but that wasn't much of a surprise to me because when I saw them eating the berries, there was probably as many as sixty to maybe as many as a hundred.

There is one experience that makes a bohemian waxwing such a funny bird or should I say more appropriately, an absolutely hilarious bird.

That is because there is a number of crab apple trees in the backyard zoo and if there are any crab apples left on the tree, they will fall off as soon as the leaves start to turn color.

Well, needless to say, the crab apples will begin to ferment and it is not too hard to realize what will happen to the bohemian waxwings when they eat some of the fruit that has fermented.

I can just imagine how funny it would be to watch so many bohemian waxwings walking around as they were drunk. I have been told by my mother that they could not walk or do anything.

Wow, that would certainly be something that is worth seeing, even funnier to watch. Yes, what a funny and amazing bird.

Dark-Eyed Junco

American Robin

Cannonball!

Anyone for a swim.

A bird feeder full of sunflower seeds or other grains is a must in order to attract birds to a backyard zoo. But what else is a must is a bird bath.

I was amazed just how many birds came to the bird bath just to take a drink of water, but it was not just to drink. It was also to get into the water and have a whole lot of fun while they were in the water.

I not only was able to take an amazing photograph of this American robin enjoying the bird bath, but I was also able to get a photograph of a blue jay in the bird bath as well. What was interesting with the blue jay was that the water was splashing so much, it was very hard even to see the blue jay. Actually, all that I could see was a hint of blue in the water.

Now that was fun!

The only regret that I have is that I didn't see to it that the backyard zoo had a bird bath for all the amazing visitors to enjoy sooner.

Yes, birds gotta have fun!

White-Breasted Nuthatch

The white-breasted nuthatch is a beautiful bird. I really enjoy how the colors go together, the bluish grey color with the white breast. Don't want to forget the tint of red that you see on them as well.

But what makes the white-breasted nuthatch a truly incredible and cute bird is the noise that they make. You can unmistakably know that you are close to a white-breasted nuthatch as you are walking around the backyard zoo because the sound that they make is like a squeak.

Yes, the white-breasted nuthatch is just like a squeak toy, a cute squeak toy.

Even though you get too close to a white-breasted nuthatch and they are busy squeaking away, it doesn't seem to bother them. Especially when they are trying to get a peanut from the feeders that are in the backyard zoo.

Yes, they are too busy going about their business getting food for themselves, while I just stand there and get some amazing photographs of them.

But I will warn you that you better be quick about taking the photograph because they will swoop in and grab a peanut and then, quickly fly away to enjoy the peanut that they had just taken.

There is something else that makes watching and photographing the amazing white-breasted nuthatch such a truly enjoyable experience.

It is the way that the white-breasted nuthatch has to sneak up to the bird feeder from time to time. You see, it starts at almost the top of the oak tree and then, it walks down the trunk of the tree. As it is walking down the trunk, it will disappear from sight as it goes to the back of the tree and then, it will reappear as it shows up on the front of the trunk. It does this back and forth until it eventually reaches its goal and then, one quick jump onto the platform. It immediately grabs a peanut and then it's gone, sometimes even before I can get a photograph.

Thankfully, for the cooperation from the white-breasted nuthatch which pauses occasionally as it walks down the trunk of the tree, I am allowed to get an amazing photograph of a white-breasted nuthatch.

Thanks a bunch!

Yellow Warbler

Yellow-Throated Vireo

House Finch

I was definitely surprised to see a house finch when it first arrived to my backyard zoo. I didn't believe that this bird would make it this far north so I was not expecting to see it as a visitor to the backyard zoo.

When I did a little research on what kind of a bird that I saw and had taken an amazing photograph of, I realized it was a house finch and I was absolutely thrilled.

Yes, another bird to enjoy and get so many amazing photographs of. It is always a thrill to see my backyard zoo expand as more and more birds, like a house finch visit the backyard zoo, even if it is for a short period of time.

It also shows that one was to be very observant as well so that you don't miss any opportunities to take an amazing photograph of an amazing bird as a house finch that maybe is here today, but not here tomorrow. They were in the backyard zoo during the fall and in the early part of one winter and I haven't seen them again.

Yes, it was really great to be able to take a photograph of a bird that I thought that I would never see in my backyard. I was also excited to see how many house finches, male and female, showed up and moved in for a while so that they can enjoy the wealth of sunflower seeds that I was feeding all the birds that showed up to visit the amazing backyard zoo.

American Goldfinch

The American goldfinch is a very striking and beautiful bird. When you see the American goldfinch display its very vivid colors, from the yellow body to its black and white wings and its orange beak and we must not forget about the black forehead and eyes, it's not that much of a surprise that so many view the American goldfinch as a bird of extraordinary beauty.

All of this vivid colors make the American goldfinch not only stand out as unique, but truly beautiful.

But what surprised me the most was that I was able to get an amazing photograph of this American goldfinch juvenile so late in the year.
Actually, the date was January 5. Yes, in the middle of winter and this amazing bird had not flown to a warmer climate. I guess this crazy bird forgot to look at his calendar or was having so much fun in the backyard zoo, it wasn't necessary to leave.

I still can't believe that I was able to get this photograph of an American goldfinch at this time of year. It took me a long time, a long time to convince myself that I was in fact seeing what I was seeing. But there it is, no argument!

Its incidents like this that make the backyard zoo such an amazing place. One can always expect the unexpected to happen. This American goldfinch is a stellar example of that phrase being true!

Of course, when one considers how small this bird is, it isn't the vivid colors that make it so noticeable as it flies over head. It is its unique sound that it makes as it is flying. It is a beautiful sound, a whistling sound. It clearly lets a person know that it is coming. Yes, it is a beautiful, melodious sound.

Then, once this beautiful bird, the American goldfinch has landed on a branch or the bird feeder, its vivid colors are now on display. Truly, it is amazing and breath taking to see this bird, the American goldfinch in all its glory.

Birds

Purple Finch

The purple finch has a very unique name because for obvious reasons it is hard to understand why a bird that is red in color has the name that it does, a purple finch. I thought that this is what made the bird so unique. Why not?

Do you know why this bird is called a purple finch?

I was definitely surprised by the answer to that question. Why this bird has the color purple in its name is because that is the color of its excrement.

I never paid much attention to this interesting fact until I began to notice the purple coloring on the rocks around the bird feeder as well as the little cedar house that I put sunflower seeds in. After seeing this, I can plainly see what the purple finch was named this way.

Yes, it is truly interesting how this bird got its name, but in spite of this, it is still a beautiful bird that gave me many hours of enjoyment.

When they first showed up in the backyard zoo, there must have been as many as twenty or more. Boy, could they make the sunflower seeds disappear in a hurry. That fact wasn't much of a surprise. After all, any bird that is given a wealth of feed is going to take advantage of it. Who wouldn't?

But I really enjoyed feeding these amazing bird, even the purple finches that showed up to the backyard zoo as this allowed me to get many amazing photographs of a purple finch.

Hoary Redpoll

When it comes to distinguishing if a redpoll is a hoary or a common one, there isn't much of a difference. Basically, the difference between the two is that a hoary redpoll has a red forehead and a common redpoll has a red cap.

That is not much of a difference.

It is because of this small difference that I have a little bit of trouble of telling which one of the redpolls is a hoary or a common one. I know that I have misnamed one of these redpolls before. Therefore, I believe that I have named these redpolls correctly.

It is still amazing how relaxed they are when it comes to approaching them. You can get quite close to them before they fly away. They seem quite natural around me and I was able to get some unbelievable close-ups of the hoary redpoll and the common redpolls as well.

It is certainly a thrill to be able to get so many amazing photographs just because these birds are so helpful and they poise so naturally for me as well.

Common Redpoll

Pine Grosbeak

Not only is a pine grosbeak a very beautiful bird with its bright red coloration on the male and the yellow coloration on the female. But it is also the sound, the beautiful music that they make when they sing. It is for this reason why I feel that a pine grosbeak is such an amazing bird. I find that they make the most melodious sound of all the birds.

When six to ten of them move into the backyard zoo, I could just sit and listen to them all day long. Yes, what an amazing bird!

The best part of watching these pine grosbeaks is that when they are eating the sunflower seeds on the platform feeder, they are so busy eating, I am able to walk right up to them and they are in no hurry to fly away. They just take a close, but quick look at me and then, they continue on with the chore at hand. EATING!

This has allowed me to get some amazing photographs and it also gave me lots of time to just watch and enjoy them when they visit the backyard zoo. Yes, these amazing birds are also big eaters and it doesn't take them very long to eat about a half a gallon of seeds. But it was certainly worth it to be able to enjoy such a beautiful bird.

Black-Billed Magpie

When we think of a black-billed magpie or for that matter, an American crow, we naturally think of what a nuisance that they are and all that they do is a whole bunch of squawking that is irritating, especially so early in the morning when we are still trying to get some sleep.

But what amazes me is that with all this against them, they are still a very beautiful looking bird.

Just take a look at this photograph of this black-billed magpie and the beautiful coloration that it possesses. Yes, to the naked eye it appears that it is just a black and white bird. But, look at the tint of blue that can be seen as well.

It really isn't such a plain and ordinary bird after all, it certainly has a wide range of color and beauty to it. Even the color black makes a bird stand out as it does for the American Crow.

Yes, it is amazing that something as ordinary as a black-billed magpie an the American crow are still an incredibly beautiful bird.

American Crow

Rose-Breasted Grosbeak

The rose-breasted grosbeak is another beautiful bird that I was privileged to have pass through my amazing zoo. Just as the sun rises every morning, so does the rose-breasted grosbeak appear every spring of the year.

The amazing colors of a rose-breasted grosbeak and the way that each color makes the others stand out so vividly makes it such a joy to watch and to photograph. Yes, it is truly beautiful how the black and white colors make the red breast so vivid and makes it stand out so distinctively. Yes, it is the colors that makes the rose-breasted grosbeak stand out so vividly!

The only regret that I have is that I wish that this amazing rose-breasted grosbeak would stay a little longer in the backyard zoo like so many of the other birds that visit. It seems to appear for, but a moment and then, just as quickly as it arrives, it disappears.

Well at any rate, for the short time that it is in the backyard zoo, I was able to enjoy and get a few amazing photographs of a rose-breasted grosbeak. I am hopeful that the next time that the rose-breasted grosbeak comes back for a visit, it will stay for a much longer stay, several weeks so that I will be able to get even more amazing photographs. You can never have enough photographs of a very beautiful bird.

Animals

Red Fox

What an amazing photograph!

One day as I looked into the backyard zoo, I saw a red fox. I have actually seen red foxes a few times, but by the time that I got my camera so that I could get a photograph, the red fox was long gone. They just do not stay long enough for me to get an amazing photograph.

But that was okay because as disappointed that I am that I could not get an amazing photograph of a red fox in my backyard zoo, I decided to put these amazing photographs of a red fox in my book. The reason is because this red fox deserves to be put into this book as well as the experience that goes with it, even though they were taken someplace else.

It is truly an amazing story and it just proved to me why changing one's mind about something from time to time is actually a very good idea.

It all started one day as I was driving down the highway on my way to Prince Albert. As I neared the town of Birch Hills, I came across a fairly large meadow that was beside the highway and I noticed a red fox.

I reasoned to myself that since I had so many amazing photographs of the red foxes that I had seen from the many times that I went to the Prince.

Albert National Park, I decided that I wasn't going to stop and take a photograph.

Well, it didn't take me long to change my mind. That I might be missing out on an amazing experience. So, I did the only thing that I could do. I turned my truck around and went back to where the red fox was, so that I could take a few photographs. Hoping that the red fox was still there by the time I got back.

Happily, to my surprise he was. So, *off* I went to get my photographs of the red fox and after I had, I came back to my truck.

When I got back, I excitedly told my mother about the amazing photograph of the red fox with its tail in the air as it had caught its meal. Then, I proceeded to watch the red fox swallowed whatever it was whole.

Naturally, my mother wanted to see the photographs and as she looked through them, she told me that I had taken a photograph of the red fox as it was jumping in the air in order to catch its food.

Well, needless to say, I was quite surprised, but I was even more excited that I had stopped to take a photograph and was able to get an amazing one at that. This proved to be a stellar day for me!

Yes, look at what I would have missed out on, if I hadn't been smart enough to change my mind. Thankfully, my love for photographing the amazing wildlife, such as a red fox made me stop to get this golden opportunity of a red fox jumping in the air.

Jack Rabbit

As we have seen so far, there is always plenty of birds that can be found in a backyard zoo. But there is also plenty of animals that show up like rabbits, whether they are bush rabbits or jack rabbits like this one.

I can remember one night when three jack rabbits came and ate the seeds that were on the ground, underneath the lighthouse bird feeder. I was even privileged to get a photograph of a jack rabbit doing this very thing.

I certainly am thrilled that these amazing jack rabbits are such a frequent visitor to the backyard zoo as it has allowed me to get so many amazing photographs of them in so many different ways. One of the amazing ways in which I look forward to getting a photograph is the various shades that their coats turn. From brown to the white coat and we must not forget about all the shades in between. Yes, I have some amazing photographs of rabbits, both jack rabbits and bush rabbits as their coat is changing colors.

I even have a photograph of a jack rabbit as it was eating dandelion leaves. Yes, you can still see part of the leaf as the jack rabbit was eating it. It definitely makes for an amazing photograph!

But what is probably the most amazing experience that I had with a jack rabbit was the time when I was sitting outside and trying to get a photograph of a bird that might come to the bird feeder.

I was absolutely amazed when I saw this jack rabbit come into the backyard zoo. Yes, not only did the jack rabbit show up, but the jack rabbit walked right between me and the platform bird feeder. He even stopped right in front of me so that I could get an amazing photograph.

Bush Rabbit

When it comes to the difference between a bush rabbit and a jack rabbit, you can certainly see the difference. A bush rabbit is smaller and I was certainly happy to get so many photographs.

At least, I hope that the photographs that I have are indeed that of a bush rabbit.

Sometimes it is hilarious that a bush rabbit thinks that it can hide from me, even though it still is out in the open. But, since I am very sneaky, it seems that they pay very little attention to what I am doing. This allows me to get very close to the bush rabbits and I am able to get some amazing photographs.

I was even able to get a photograph of a bush rabbit as it was way too busy eating the pine needles that had fallen to the ground. Again, what a thrill it is to get so close that I can even get an amazing head shot of this beautiful and amazing bush rabbit.

American Red Squirrel

The American red squirrel can be described very appropriately by just two little words, agile and feisty. Yes, it is certainly amazing how the American red squirrel can run up and down a tree so fast and can jump from branch to branch with such ease. I am simply in awe as I watch this amazing American red squirrel.

But, with all the amazing agility that this American red squirrel possesses, it doesn't help him when it comes to protecting his food supply from the many birds that come to the backyard zoo. But, more about this later.

It is certainly amazing to watch an American red squirrel as he runs up a tree in order to store peanuts in a very good place of his choosing. When I consider how many times that he runs up the tree, I am beginning to think that his hiding place should eventually get full. The American red squirrel must have bags and bags of seeds up in the tree, but he still keeps going up and down with what appears to be no end in sight.

What an amazing and industrious worker!

I am beginning to wonder if the birds are raiding his stash and that is probably why the hiding place for his peanuts never seem to get full. Yes, the American red squirrel is obviously in amazing physical shape so that the American red squirrel can get his food stored away for the winter.

There is something else that makes watching the American red squirrel such a joy is that even though, there is more than enough seeds for everyone who visit the backyard zoo, birds and all. The american red squirrel obvious thinks that all the peanuts and seeds are all his. He is naturally and definitely not interested in sharing. Yes just look at him.

So, when a bird dares to try and get some seeds to eat, the American red squirrel chases them away. It doesn't matter if the birds are on the pine trees or the oak tree, neither does it matter who the bird is either.

From a blue jay to a black-billed magpie to a house sparrow, even a little red-breasted nuthatch or a black-capped chickadee has to be chased away. But the birds are just as smart as the American red squirrel is.

You see, as soon as the American red squirrel chases the birds off one branch, they simply fly to another branch. Then, when they are chased off that branch, they will just fly back to the previous branch that they were on. It seems like a perpetual exercise, but that doesn't seem to bother the American red squirrel all that much. I'm beginning to think that the American red squirrel is enjoying the unproductive exercise of trying to chase the birds away. I am thrilled at the privilege of watching this unfold before my very eyes. Amazing!

Obviously, the birds don't really mind either or are bothered that much by being chased by the American red squirrel. They must know that eventually, the American red squirrel will give up the chase and go back to storing the peanuts in the pine tree that is just behind the oak tree.

Now, their time has arrived and no matter what bird it is, whether it is a blue jay or a red-breasted nuthatch their patience has paid off. Yes, as the American red squirrel runs up the tree with a peanut, it is now the birds turn to get filled up with peanuts and sunflower seeds.

One day I noticed that the bell made out of sunflower seeds was laying on the ground. When I went over to hang it back up, I saw that the plastic hook was chewed off. I guess, the American red squirrel was tired of hanging onto a branch upside down while eating the seeds of the bell. Naturally, it is much easier to eat the seeds when they are on the ground.

Funny though, when there was already a lot of sunflower seeds on the ground. So, why was the American red squirrel continually making sure that the bell was on the ground?

Puzzling, at least to me it was, but not to the American red squirrel. He obviously has a plan.

One day as I was trying to get an amazing photograph of another bird that appeared in the backyard zoo, which I will talk about later. It was at this time that I came to realize what the American red squirrel was up to, his diabolical plan.

Why the bell had to be on the ground, at least from his perspective.

Imagine that this American red squirrel was trying to get that bell, which by the way was as big as he is, either up the tree for storage or to his nest. Whatever he was doing with it, he was not going to give up. Later on, I noticed that the bell was gone. Yes, success at last!

All that work must have paid off for this amazing American red squirrel. Simply, amazing! What an animal!

Mule Deer

The mule deer and a white-tailed deer are so similar that sometimes it is hard to tell them apart. It is for this reason that I almost put this photograph of a mule deer with my amazing photographs of a white-tailed deer.

But, as I took a closer look at the tail, I came to realize that this had to be a mule deer. The tail of a mule deer is certainly different from the white tail of a white-tailed deer. The tail of a mule deer as a black tip and the tail of a whitetailed deer pops up as it runs away.

White-Tailed Deer

One thing that I look forward to every year is the arrival of the white-tailed deer. They appear in the backyard zoo every winter. I have seen from as many as five to seven white-tailed deer.

It must have been the two huge crab apple trees that drew these amazing white-tailed deer to the backyard. Yes, they got into the habit of eating the crab apples and they must really have enjoyed the crab apples. Even though, there was two huge crab apple trees that were loaded with fruit, I couldn't find one single crab apple left on the ground by the time that spring rolled around.

One thing about any animal, even a white-tailed deer is that they are smart as they are quick to learn about how to get their food.

A prime example of this was when they lost one food source, they soon look for another way to get their food. The crab apple trees produced so much fruit that with time, the branches snapped from the weight of all that fruit. So, it became necessary to cut those trees down.

Now, that they had no fruit to eat, they would have to look elsewhere to satisfy their hunger. Well, it didn't take them long to find the bird feeders that were in the backyard.

It was actually quite hilarious to watch the white-tailed deer trying to get at the bird seed. I will have to admit that one of the white-tailed deer was really smart as she soon was able to figure out that by pushing on the lighthouse bird feeder, the seeds would come running out of it. This made it really easy to get a good meal, plus it saved them a lot of time as well.

But, one thing that they could not figure out which made them so funny to watch was that they must have thought there was an unlimited supply of seeds in the bird feeder.

When it was obvious that the bird feeder was empty, the white-tailed deer were not convinced of this because they would then take their frustration out on the bird feeder by bunting the bird feeder with their nose.

It was quite amusing watching them try and try to get seeds from an empty bird feeder, seeing it swing like a pendulum as they were hitting it with their nose. Now, that was funny!

Yes, it was certainly enjoyable to watch these very amazing white-tailed deer.

Birds

Merlin

I have already mentioned what some people would consider an unwanted visitor to the backyard zoo and in some sense, they might be right.

One of these unwelcome visitors is definitely a merlin. That is because of one simple reason, they scare all the other birds away. They are very disruptive to my amazing backyard zoo.

Yes, they are quite an amazing bird, but for one simple reason that they like to use other birds as food. But, one thing about a merlin is that they are not always successful in catching their food.

One time that I can remember is when a merlin appeared in the backyard zoo and he tried twice to catch a house sparrow and failed both times. Even this merlin sitting in this pine tree wasn't having much success. Yes, with all the birds that were in the backyard zoo, all this merlin could do was sit in the tree and eye all the other birds that were in the tree. Sitting on the branches. Safe from the harm that the merlin can bring them.

Sharp-Shinned Hawk

I mentioned before how disappointing it was when a bird of prey came into the backyard zoo and chased all the red crossbills away, so that I was unable to take any more photographs of this amazing bird.

Well, it was a sharp-shinned hawk that was able to catch a bird in midair as I was sitting and watching the red crossbills eating the sunflower seeds on the platform bird feeder. I knew that the sharp-shinned hawk was successful because it landed on the snow not that far away from the pine trees. After, the sharp-shinned hawk had taken a look at what he was able to catch and realizing that it was now dead, the sharp-shinned hawk flew away.

To say that I was disappointed, is a gross understatement. I was certainly saddened for this to have happened in my backyard zoo. But there is nothing that I could have done about this. It had happened just too fast.

I am certainly thankful that as good as a sharp-shinned hawk is in catching its prey, it is not always successful as one experience has taught me and I am thrilled about this.

It all happened one day as I was watching a blue jay eating peanuts from the platform feeder. The blue jay would take a peanut and then, fly into the oak tree to eat it. When the blue jay went to get another peanut, he didn't land on the platform feeder. The blue jay just flew into the lilac hedge instead.

When the blue jay didn't stay long in the lilac hedge, but flew out of the backyard zoo, I quickly came to realize why the blue jay was acting in such a peculiar way. What only one peanut, then gone!

Yes, in just a few seconds after the blue jay had flown away, I saw a sharpshinned hawk flying into the backyard zoo. Since the sharp-shinned hawk realized that it would not going to catch the blue jay, it turned its attention to the many house sparrows that were sitting in the lilac hedge.

That was a poorly thought out decision as the sharp-shinned hawk got hung up in the lilac hedge. Yes, what goes around, come around.

It was really funny to see the sharp-shinned hawk with its butt in the air and it took him a considerable amount of time to get out from the branches that he was caught in. When the sharp-shinned hawk finally managed to get out, it just sat there on a branch and this allowed me to get many photographs.

Obviously, the sharp-shinned hawk must have been dazed because he sat for so long on the branch. Well, one thing that I now know is how a small bird must feel when a sharp-shinned hawk is chasing him. This experience even shook me up and I was watching from the safety of a house.

Animals

Coyote

For as often that I can hear a coyote at night, I have rarely seen one. I have heard as many as three coyote howling one night. But that is a good thing because a coyote can also be very disruptive to a backyard zoo.

I can remember one night when I could hear our pet dog just barking his head off, so I headed outside to see what was going on and I was sure glad that I had.

Here was a coyote in the backyard zoo, obviously eyeing up the dog for its next meal. Boy, I was sure glad that the dog was tied up on his leash.

But, this wasn't the first time that I saw a coyote near the backyard zoo. I actually saw two coyote getting a bead on the neighbor's dog. But, since this dog was also tied up, the two coyote gave up in trying to get the dog to leave the safety of the yard and left.

This was certainly an interesting exercise to watch these two coyotes work as a team in trying to get this dog. At least, I was able to get a photograph of one of the coyote as it walked towards the dog.

But, as is the case with any wild animal, if they are hungry enough, they will go to were the food is. As we have seen so far, a coyote is usually looking at other animals or birds as their source for food. But what I have come to realize that is not always the case. Food after all is food, even if it is bird seeds.

Yes, when a coyote is hungry enough, they will eat anything, even the sunflower seeds on a platform feeder.

As is the case every morning, I put out more seeds for the many birds that will show up during the day. Most of the time, I just have to add to what is left over from the previous day as the birds don't always eat everything that is on the platform feeder.

But, one day when I went to fill up the bird feeders, I noticed that the platform was, as the expression goes, licked clean. I really didn't think much of it at the time, because I just thought that a white-tailed deer had shown up, but since I could hear the coyote howling at night, we kept an eye open for one.

That is because of our pet dog and therefore, we would check to see if any coyote was in the yard before we let the dog out at night. Well, one night when I looked outside, I was very surprised that I saw a coyote near the platform where I had the sunflower seeds.

Wow, that coyote must have been very hungry. To have settled on the sunflower seeds that were on the platform. Now, I know why it had nothing on it. The coyote was now a regular visitor to the backyard zoo, but only after the sun had gone down. Still, I was able to get a pretty good photograph of him at the platform as my mother was shining a flashlight on him.

As the days went by, the coyote seemed to be getting more and more brave as I was able to go outside during the day and here the coyote was at the platform feeder. Maybe, the coyote was just that hungry or that desperate.

Whatever the case, I was allowed to get an amazing photograph of the coyote as he tried to sneak up on the platform feeder without being seen. It didn't work for him, I spotted him anyway.

From my viewpoint, what an incredible and beautiful animal.

Naturally, I kept my eye open for another opportunity to get an amazing photograph. I was indeed grateful that I was able to get one of the coyote as he sat on a snow drift in the neighbor's backyard. I just sat down on the ground and watched him as the coyote watched me. I guess the coyote thought that I was a pest because I was preventing him from getting to the sunflower seeds. Yes, I was in the way of the coyote eating.

What was really enjoyable was the fact that he caused me no harm, all that the coyote was concerned about was his next meal, even if it was sunflower seeds. After all, who isn't?

Sometimes the wildlife gets a bit of a bad reputation. Sometimes it is deserved and not deserved. Well, anyways I have certainly enjoyed watching such a beautiful animal. Who would have thought?

Beehive

What an amazing piece of engineering!

Yes, when I opened the door to the shed and then, was able to see inside a beehive. I had no choice, but to put it in the book about the amazing backyard zoo. The decision was really easy to make.

When we look at the inside of a beehive, we can certainly see just how intricate they really are. Yes, it was indeed a very special privilege to be able to look inside of a beehive in this way.

What amazing builder the bee really is!

One thing that makes my backyard zoo such an amazing place is that because there are no cages and fences, any bird or animal can just come right on in and enjoy the abundance of seeds that are available to them.

So this year was a very exciting year for the backyard zoo as I was able to get amazing photographs of nine different birds that made a visit to the backyard zoo.

One of the amazing birds that showed up was a clay-colored sparrow like this one.

It is certainly a very enjoyable experience to find so many new and different birds, some of which I have never seen before, show up in the backyard zoo.

I was even able to get so many amazing photograph of birds that I didn't even expect to see in my backyard zoo. One of this birds was a common grackle and the biggest surprise of all, mallard ducklings. Yes, I don't even have a pond in my backyard zoo and here there were, just waddling along through the backyard zoo.

So, I hope that you will enjoy the new attractions to the backyard zoo as it expands with even more impressive attraction with each and every passing year.

Clay-Colored Sparrow

This is one of the amazing birds that showed up in my backyard zoo that I had never seen before until it came to enjoy the grains that I put out to feed the birds.

What a beautiful looking sparrow. I am thrilled that this amazing claycolored sparrow took the time to visit the backyard zoo. I am in awe at the coloring of a clay-colored sparrow with the tan coloring and then, there is the color white blended in. Wow, what a beautiful bird and a sparrow at that!

It is the most beautiful looking sparrow to show up in the backyard zoo. I am hoping that this incredibly looking clay-colored sparrow will be a regular visitor because I really am looking forward to seeing this amazing clay-colored sparrow every year!

Lincoln's Sparrow

This was the second sparrow that showed up to the backyard zoo this year. I was thrilled that this amazing Lincoln's sparrow also took the time to drop in for a visit.

Yes, just like a clay-colored sparrow, a Lincoln's sparrow is a beautiful looking bird. When you look at the array of color that you see, how these colors blend together and highlight the other colors as well. It just shows what a beautiful bird it is in its own right. Yes, the Lincoln's sparrow is a beauty!

I am absolutely thrilled that I was able to get so close to both of these amazing birds, the Lincoln's sparrow and the clay-colored sparrow, that it allowed me to get such amazing photographs.

That is one reason why I love to just sit outside and enjoy the amazing backyard zoo. I am certainly appreciative for all the help that I get from time to time so that I can get such amazing photographs. But, it really isn't that hard as it is the wildlife that make the photograph so amazing.

Yellow-rumped Warbler

This is one of two warblers that showed up to the backyard zoo this year. The other one was an orange-crowned warbler. I am thrilled that I was fortunate enough that on the day they arrived, I was outside so that I could get an amazing photograph of the both of them.

This yellow-rumped warbler that I was able to get an amazing photograph of is a juvenile.

Orange-Crowned Warbler

Swainson's Thrush

I was thrilled that this incredible bird, a Swainson's thrush was also a visitor to the backyard zoo. But it was funny just how shy this bird was when the Swainson's thrush showed up.

Most birds just head to the various feeders and begin to eat, all that they want. But, the Swainson's thrush would try to sneak up to the seeds.

This was probably because in my zeal to get an amazing photograph of the birds that were in the backyard zoo, I was probably too close to the feeders.

Obviously, the actions of the Swainson's thrush did not discourage me nor did they stop me from getting an amazing photograph of a Swainson's thrush.

I was very thankful that the Swainson's thrush was so cautious as I was allowed to get some amazing photograph as these incredible birds were standing on a rock. It certainly made for a prettier photograph having the rocks in the photograph. I was thrilled!

Common Grackle

To the naked eye, we don't get to see just how beautiful a common grackle is. Yes, to the naked eye all that you notice is its bluish purple head, but you can't see just how colorful the rest of the feathers are. What beauty!

Even though, a common grackle makes for an amazing photograph and I have found much enjoyment in photographing them, it is the sound that they make when I am too close to the feeder. It is an interesting sound to say the least, but a very melodious one at that.

Yes, they are an incredible bird and when you put their bluish purple head with their bronze looking body together, you can see why they are an aweinspiring bird to look at and to photograph.

Just another bird that makes the backyard zoo such an amazing place to enjoy and makes me glad that I have seen to setting up such a place.

Birds

Rusty Blackbird

When you hear the name rusty blackbird, you soon realize that it really isn't black in color, but a closer look at the rusty blackbird and you soon realize that there is a tint of blue in the feathers.

Yes, it doesn't matter what bird that we are talking about, a closer look reveals that one color just won't do. What makes a bird truly beautiful is the array of colors that can be found on a bird, even if it is a tint of blue that can be found on the rusty blackbird.

Philadelphia Vireo

Mallard Ducklings

To my surprise and amazement, a mallard duck and her ducklings came waddling across the yard.

As soon as I got outside so that I could take a photograph of them, the mother flew away to my surprise. The mother had left her ducklings all by themselves. But at least, I was able to get a photograph of her ducklings.

The ducklings were sure cute as they tried to waddle away as quickly as they could.

To my surprise, this is not the only time that I have seen mallard ducks in the backyard zoo. I have seen a mallard, male and female, many times before in the backyard zoo.

The only regret that I have is that I don't have a considerable sized pond so that I could enjoy many different kinds of ducks and then, I would be able to take many amazing photographs.

Flowers

Something that is really noticeable about a zoo, besides the amazing animals that can be enjoyed, is the beautiful gardens that they have full of beautiful flowers.

Therefore, I thought that my backyard zoo should also have a beautiful garden. My mother has such a garden. I certainly hope that you get as much enjoyment at looking at these beautiful flowers as I did in photographing them.

Yes, there are so many beautiful flowers to enjoy such as tulips and pansies to African daisies and lilies. Even the sunflowers are truly remarkable as they have brought so much pleasure to our neighbor.

I was even able to take a photograph of a sunflower that had some fifty or more flowers. These flowers make for a truly amazing photograph in which to enjoy.

Allium

Poppy

African Daisy

Pansy

Sunflower

Lavatera

Bleeding Hearts

Lily

Tulips

Poppy

Impatience

Rose

Aster Flower

Now, let's get back to the amazing birds and animals that have just arrived to my amazing backyard. Yes, another year has come and gone and I have saved some of the best for last.

Chipmunk

One of the most surprising animal to find its way into my backyard zoo was this very cute chipmunk. I have never seen a chipmunk before in the backyard zoo, but I was certainly shocked and definitely thrilled to see the chipmunk show up.

Actually, I have seen a chipmunk only once before. It was while I was on vacation at Waskesiu Lake in the Prince Albert National Park. I was certainly surprised that I was able to see a chipmunk and since I had never seen a chipmunk up to this point, I was thrilled for the privilege that I had come across one so that I could get an amazing photograph.

Yes, as thrilled as I was in seeing a chipmunk, I never thought that I would ever see one in the backyard zoo. I would never have imagined it. But the day finally came when this incredible visitor showed up. Wow, what a thrill!

It all happened one day as I was outside looking to see what was in my backyard zoo so that I could take some photographs. My mother noticed that an animal was eating sunflower seeds that were under the platform feeder.

Of course, we just assumed it was an American red squirrel as it was a frequent visitor. But to my amazement, here it was a chipmunk.

Unbelievable!

I was so excited to find a chipmunk at Waskesiu Lake, and now I have a chipmunk show up right in my backyard zoo. WOW!!

Needless to say, I spent quite a few days, probably weeks sitting and watching for the next time the chipmunk arrived so that I could get some amazing photographs.

As I sat and watched this amazing creature, it was amazing to see the chipmunk fill his cheeks full of seeds. I was even able to get a photograph of the chipmunk with his cheeks almost bursting at the seams. It made me wonder, just how many seeds a chipmunk could put into its cheeks.

This summer I shingled my parents' roof, which isn't of interest. What is of interest and amazing was the fact that while every other bird and even the American red squirrel was scared away from all the hammering of the nails as I put the shingles on. Yet to my surprise, it didn't frighten the chipmunk away.

It was busier than ever, it obviously was too busy to worry about the noise as it had to get prepared for what was waiting him, WINTER!

Yes, for the short time that the chipmunk appeared in my backyard zoo, he was certainly amazing and entertaining to watch and photograph. I would be thrilled if the chipmunk showed up next year to the backyard zoo.

Birds

Song Sparrow

No matter how many times that I go outside to admire my backyard zoo, I am constantly amazed that I continue to see new and exciting birds as they stop by for a visit and to get filled up with sunflower seeds. Yes, it is absolutely thrilling to see a song sparrow as well as an American tree sparrow, even though they rarely visit my backyard zoo.

I always expect to see the common sparrows, like house sparrows or whitethroated sparrows and white-crowned sparrow, that come by every year. But it is certainly nice to see certain sparrows, like this song sparrow, so that I can see and photograph them from time to time.

But at any rate, I have enjoyed the amazing photographs of a song sparrow and the American tree sparrow when they just drop by for a short visit.

American Tree Sparrow

Red-Winged Blackbird

When one sees a red-winged blackbird, it always seems to be by a pond.

Sitting on the cattails that are found along the edge of the water. That is why I would never have thought that I would ever see a red-winged blackbird in the backyard zoo.

To my surprise, I noticed this bird sitting on the platform feeder and it waseating the sunflower seeds. Yes, a red-winged blackbird made a visit and I was able to add this amazing bird to the backyard zoo.

The only problem was that as soon as I was spotted, the red-winged blackbird flew away. Well, now that the red-winged blackbird had made an appearance, I also knew that this amazing bird would be back again and again.

This would give me many opportunities to get my amazing photograph as it feasted on the abundance of sunflower seeds.

Happily, I was indeed able to get an amazing photograph of a male and a female red-winged blackbird. What a pleasure and joy it was for me to be able to add a red-winged blackbird to my backyard zoo.

What an incredible find, simply an amazing opportunity for me.

Animal

Raccoon

What a thrill! I found it unbelievable that a raccoon made a visit to the amazing backyard zoo.

Yes, here they were. Five of them, a whole family probably and they just came in to enjoy the sunflower seeds that were on the platform feeder and the cedar house filled with sunflower seeds as well.

It was quite funny because before I realized that these raccoons had appeared in the backyard, I noticed that the bell made of sunflower seeds had disappeared and I wasn't really sure why. I thought that the American redsquirrel had taken it. Then, I saw the raccoons. I even saw a raccoon trying toget at the bell that was hanging on one of the oak tree branches.

Aha! So that is what happened to the bell.

Even though, they showed up when it was dark, it was a delight being able to watch them. I even tried to take a photograph of them, but the photograph didn't turn out very good as the photograph of the white-tailed deer that was taken at night as well clearly showed.

That is why I decided to put these amazing photographs of the raccoon in a nearby field that I was able to get, but I will talk about that later.

It was really cute when one of the raccoons stood on its back legs as it ate the sunflower seeds from the cedar house. Then, every once and a while, the raccoon would take a look towards the house as my mother had a flashlight shining on them. We did this in the hopes of getting a photograph of them.

I ended up watching them for about thirty minutes or longer. It was quite a thrill, but I sure wished that they had shown up during the day so that I could get an amazing photograph. There is always the hope, the hope that they will show up some afternoon.

As I wait patiently for this to happen, I was thrilled that I was able to get an amazing photograph of this incredible raccoon.

I have spent hours and days trying to get a photograph of a raccoon. They are just so cute-looking, it must be the mask. Yes, as hard as I tried to get a photograph I was beginning to think that this was never going to happen. I was getting more and more disappointed.

It seemed that the only raccoon I was ever going to see was a dead one. But finally, that changed in a remarkable and thrilling way. I was coming home from a very special day at the Prince Albert National Park when I saw a raccoon along a row of trees by a dugout.

I stop the truck and tried to get a photograph, but the raccoon disappeared before I could get there. But the good news was that I had finally found a raccoon and now I was going to go back the next day so that I could try and get a photograph.

Well, I went back and saw nothing. I went back again and again, but I still could not find the raccoon. Now what?

I decided to try one last time to get my photograph, but for some reason I took the long way around. As I was driving down the gravel road, I noticed two common ravens sitting out in the field. I didn't really pay much attention to what they were doing, but I was going to stop anyway to see what was going on.

Since the common ravens were so far away from the road, I took a look through the camera. Wow! Here I thought the common ravens were just by a pile of dirt and to my delight, it was a raccoon.

Off I went. As I was walking through the field so that I could get my photograph, I began to wonder if it was a dead raccoon. Thankfully, it was alive. Finally, I got my amazing photograph of a raccoon. The raccoon was obviously looking for something under the snow.

After a while, the raccoon started to walk away. That was not going to work for me, so I whistled at the raccoon to get his attention. I was certainly glad that I did as I was able to get an amazing photograph of the raccoon as it took its defensive position as the photograph shows. Wow, what an amazing pose!

After the raccoon posed for me and I took advantage of this golden opportunity. The raccoon walked back to the spot where he was digging in the snow. I continued to take many more photographs. I even watched him for quite some time after I had finished taking the photographs.

I started back for the truck and I was so excited that I had finally got my amazing photograph of a raccoon, I started to run back to the truck. For those who have tried to run in deep snow, it wasn't much of an idea. I fell in a snow drift. Oops!

As I was falling down, I landed on my back so that my camera would not be damaged. Can you imagine me like a turtle on its back trying to get up? Well, it wasn't pretty!

It took me quite some time to get up. After all, I had a camera in one hand and no gloves on. It would have been hilarious if anyone was looking at me trying to get up. But I was finally able to get to my feet and I spent the rest of the walk back to the truck laughing at myself. What an idiot!

At any rate, the only thing that mattered was that I got an amazing photograph of a raccoon. YAHOO!!

Birds

Eastern Phoebe

The eastern phoebe only made a brief appearance, extremely brief stopover to the backyard zoo.

I just happened to be sitting outside at the time and an eastern phoebe came flying in and landed on the branch of an oak tree. I was certainly thrilled that the eastern phoebe stayed on the branch for but a few seconds, just long enough for me to take one or two photographs.

As quickly as the eastern phoebe flew in, it left just as quickly. I was very fortunate that at least one of the photographs turned out. It is certainly a thrill that I was able to get an amazing photograph of an eastern phoebe, even though it was for only a brief moment.

Evening Grosbeak

Unbelievable!!!

This was another bird that I never expected to see in the backyard zoo. I was amazed when an evening grosbeak came to enjoy the sunflower seeds and the bird bath as well.

With the arrival of the evening grosbeak, the only grosbeak left to visit the backyard zoo is a black-headed grosbeak. It sure would be nice if a blackheaded grosbeak would show up next year to the amazing backyard zoo.

Now, back to the amazing evening grosbeak. Yes, as you look at this beautiful bird, it was a thrill for me to photograph this incredible bird. Yes, were does one start.

There is just so many different colors that make this evening grosbeak such a beautiful bird. It's very dark gray head and shoulders and its yellow eyebrow are features that make this bird stand out. Yes, even the black wings with white wing patches also add to the beauty of this amazing evening grosbeak.

It certainly is a joy to see so many new birds visit the backyard zoo, thus giving me so many amazing photographs.

Eurasian Collared-Dove

Not only was it a surprise to see a Eurasian collared-dove in the backyard zoo, but can you imagine my surprise when I saw four Eurasian collared-dove.

Yes, this Eurasian collared-dove is the prize and the joy of the backyard zoo.

This is for a couple of reasons. The main reason is because this bird really isn't supposed to be seen this far north. But I am not going to be too terribly concerned about this fact. The only thing that matters to me is that the Eurasian collared-dove showed up in my backyard zoo.

What a thrill and privilege to have this amazing bird visit the zoo.

Yes, they visit the backyard zoo every day to enjoy the sunflower seeds. I am very thrilled that there are four Eurasian collared-dove that show up at one time. But, the only problem or should I say concerned that I have, is that these birds are extremely hard to get a photograph.

I have sat for hours and hours, but they rarely appear in the backyard when I am sitting outside. When they do appear, they land in the trees that are behind the pine trees. I can see them walking around on the branches, but they will just not appear in the open so that I can take a photograph. Once in a while, they will land on the ground so that I can finally see them, but they are always in the shade of the trees. Naturally, the photographs will not turn out to be good enough.

Even when I see them outside, they quickly fly into the trees when I try to sneak up on them.

One time I was sitting in a patio swing that is right beside the bird feeder when an Eurasian collared-dove landed to get some seeds, but as soon as I was seen it flew back into the trees.

Ever patient, I waited for my next opportunity as I am confident that it will eventually come my way.

Happily, it did. I placed myself in such a way so that I was mostly hidden from view. It worked. In time they flew into the pine trees behind the bird feeder. They obviously were not too sure it was safe. They sat in the tree for quite some time, but eventually they flew down to the feeder in order to eat.

Bubbling over with joy, I was able to get some amazing photographs of my pride and joy, the Eurasian collared-dove.

Common Raven

There is always something that is unique and special when it comes to a zoo. This is done to attract as many guests to the zoo as possible.

So, I thought it would be prudent and wise if I could also find something unusual that would be an attraction. There is nothing as amazing as a solar pillar. You will have to agree with me that a solar pillar is very unique because you don't see one very often.

I am fifty- two years old and I have only seen such an amazing event as a solar pillar only once in my lifetime. What a thrill it was to see such an incredible phenomenon. Yes, a solar pillar is a very uncommon event. That is why I was absolutely amazed that I was able to experience such a thing as this first hand.

I was able to enjoy such a spectacular event because for me there is nothing as beautiful as a sunset. I was thrilled that I took advantage of the golden opportunity one evening when it looked like it was going to be an amazing sunset. So, off I went.

I could tell that something truly unique and incredible was about to happen when the sun was beginning to go behind the horizon.

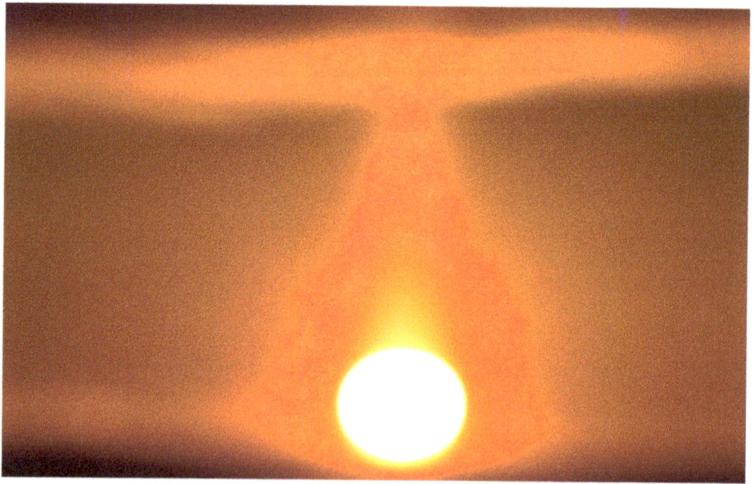

So, I immediately began to take some photographs. I was amazed and thrilled to learn later that what I had just experienced was a solar pillar. ENJOY THIS AMAZING EVENT. A SOLAR PILLAR!!!!

Solar Pillar

As big and impressive that a zoo can get, there is always a desire to make it bigger. That is certainly my desire that even more unique and amazing wildlife will visit the amazing backyard zoo. I do have a wish list, so to speak.

Yes, for as many amazing wildlife that I have been so privilege to watch and photograph in my parents' backyard, it has been quite an experience. But there is always certain amazing wildlife that I wish would stop by and visit this amazing zoo.

There are six other birds on my wish list, that stand out as amazing. These incredible birds that I hope will come into my backyard zoo stand out for various reasons such as their majesty or for their sheer beauty. Whatever the reason, it would be a thrill if they did come by. Even though, it is unlikely.

What a thrill if a palm warbler would make the backyard zoo his home.

What an incredible bird, the sheer beauty of this amazing bird with its variety of colors.

Palm Warbler

Here is the rest of my list.

       1- Bald Eagle

       2- Snowy Owl

       3- Pied- billed Grebe

       4- Yellow headed Blackbird

Naturally, the pleasure that I find in watching and photographing the amazing wildlife that has been in the backyard zoo thus far has caused me to take a great deal of photographs. Therefore, I thought that I should limit my list.

As you can see from my list, a few of them are easy and obvious to select. The bald eagle and the snowy owl are in themselves a truly stunning and majestic when you see and experience them in the wild.

Bald Eagle

The bald eagle is such a majestic bird and the snowy owl stand alone as my favorite owl. Wow! Words fail when it comes to describing these amazing birds.

The pied-billed grebe is also a favorite of mine as I have found just how playful they really are. Finally, the fifth but certainly not any less impressive is the yellow-headed blackbird and how it puts its whole body into making its unique, but amazing sound.

It is certainly my desire that you find these incredible birds as amazing as I do.

Snowy Owl

Pied-Billed Grebe

Yellow-Headed Blackbird

Common Nighthawk

The common nighthawk is the sixth amazing bird on my list of birds that I hope will visit the amazing backyard zoo. Actually, I have only seen this amazing looking bird just once and I almost missed seeing him.

The reason why the common nighthawk makes my list is because even though, it is very menacing looking, I think it is a remarkable looking bird.

As you can see, I was able to get an amazing photograph of this common nighthawk as it was resting on the railroad tracks. I almost missed it as I was walking to coffee. I just happened to look towards the railroad tracks and saw that something was there.

Naturally, I went to see what it was and here it was a bird. I had no idea what it was, but I took my photographs. I was really thrilled that I was able to get so close to this incredible common nighthawk before it flew away.
I am very thankful that my eyes are constantly roving about just in case I am able to find something in which to take a photograph of, an amazing photograph of a common nighthawk, for instance.

It has been a privilege to give you a tour of this amazing backyard zoo and all the amazing wildlife that can be found there. I also have been privileged to watch and to take so many amazing photographs of these incredible wildlife.

I am thrilled that I can end my tour on a couple of amazing experiences. I have already mentioned that I was able to get a photograph of a raccoon, but it was at night and that I was sure hopeful that the raccoon would show up during the day to eat the sunflower seeds.

Hooray! Hooray! The raccoon showed up during the day, finally!

Here I was standing right beside the platform feeder when this amazing raccoon showed up. Yes, I was only two feet away from the feeder and this raccoon cautiously took a peek from behind the oak tree. Looking at me, wondering if it was safe enough to come and eat the sunflower seeds.

It was and boy, was I glad that I had my 15-55 mm lens so that I could get these amazing photographs. What a way to end the tour of the amazing backyard zoo.

Yes, if you are patient enough, the rewards are amazing and incredible. But that is not all. There is a reason why I had my 15-55 mm lens on as I also have some thrilling news in which to relate with regards to a black-capped chickadee and a red-breasted nuthatch.

I wonder if the guy with the camera will give me a hand up. I guess not!

Ever since I was able to feed some very special friends from the Prince Albert National Park, the gray jays from my hand. I have been trying and trying, again and again to feed the birds that show up in the backyard zoo from my hand.

As you have seen, I have come close a couple of times, but the day finally arrived and I was able to feed a bird some peanuts from my hand. The first one to take a peanut was a red-breasted nuthatch.

What a thrill! To say that I was grinning from ear to ear was a gross understatement. What a joy it is to have these very beautiful and precious birds take a peanut from your hand.

What was amazing was that the red-breasted nuthatch was not hesitant at all when it came to taking a peanut from my hand. But what was even more rewarding was that the red-breasted nuthatch took his time. He paused for a while and just stood there for a few seconds on my hand.

Yes, the red-breasted nuthatches did not just grab or snatch a peanut and then, fly away. This allowed me to take my time when it came to taking an amazing photograph. What an amazing photograph that I was able to get of an incredible and beautiful bird, the red-breasted nuthatch.

Yes, another friend!!!

I am very happy to say that a red-breasted nuthatch was not the only bird that I was able to take a peanut from my hand. Yes, now that the floodgates were open It was a thrill to see so many birds taking a peanut from my hand. Yes I was even able to get a black capped chickadee to land on my hand.

But, not just one black-capped chickadee as I was able to count five, maybe six black-capped chickadees taking peanuts from my hand. were open it was a thrill to see so many birds taking a peanut from my hand.

Yes, I was even able to get a black-capped chickadee to land on my hand.

Yes, it was quite a thrill to see so many birds taking peanuts from my hand. Just as soon as one left, another one came and took a peanut and the cycle seems to be endless. What a thrill!

I certainly have something amazing to look forward to everyday. Yes, the amazing backyard just keeps on getting better and better with every passing day. I don't know what else I can look forward to next year.

Well, I certainly hope that you have enjoyed the tour of this amazing backyard and if you would like this same kind of a backyard like this amazing one, all you need is a whole lot of bird seeds, especially sunflower seeds and peanuts and the beautiful birds and all the amazing animals will find your amazing backyard zoo as well.

It is always special to end the day with fireworks! Everybody love fireworks.

220

THE
END